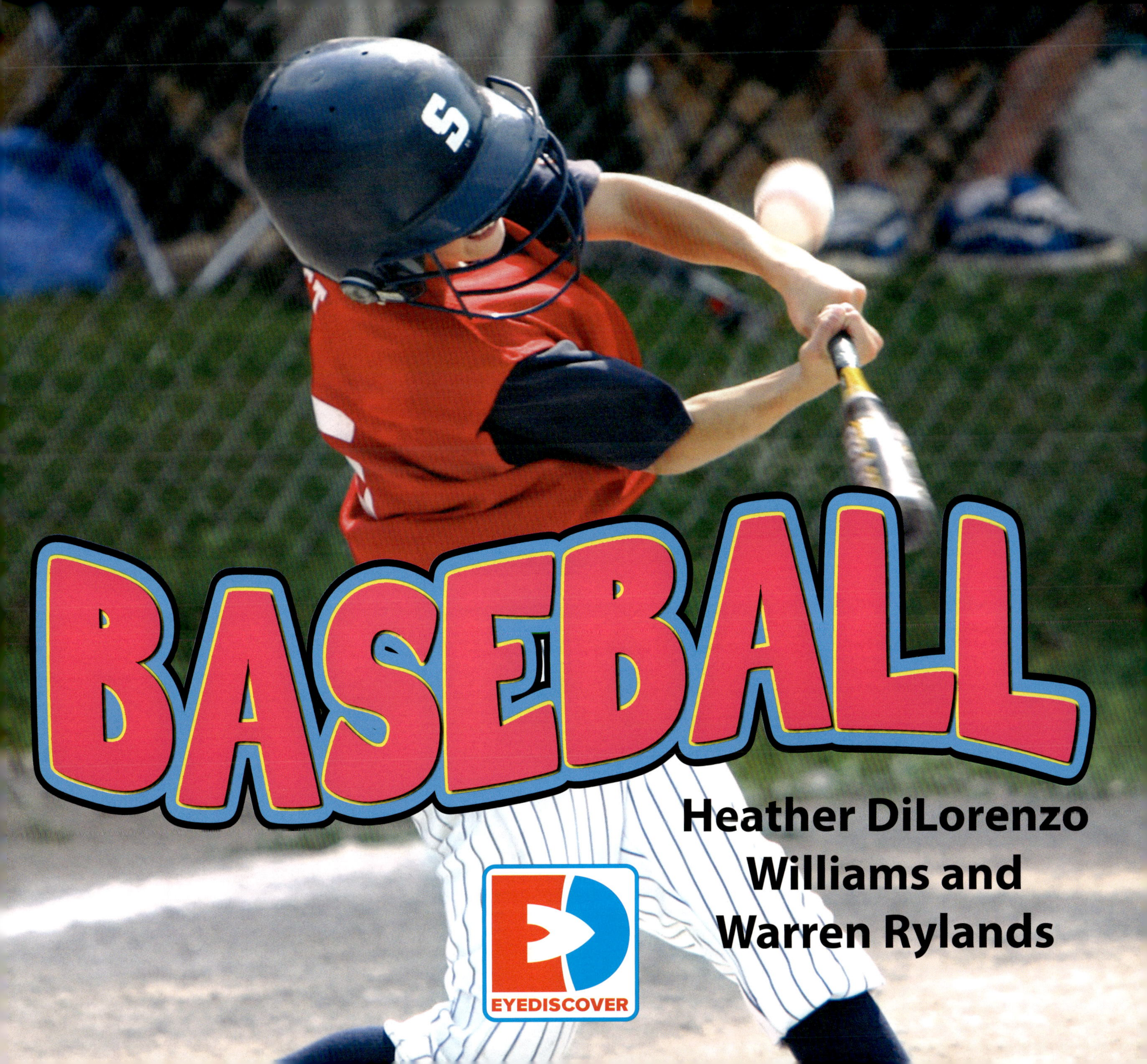

BASEBALL

Heather DiLorenzo Williams and Warren Rylands

EYEDISCOVER

Go to **www.eyediscover.com** and enter this book's unique code.

BOOK CODE

AVQ56868

EYEDISCOVER brings you optic readalongs that support active learning.

Published by AV² by Weigl
350 5th Avenue, 59th Floor New York, NY 10118
Website: www.eyediscover.com

Library of Congress Control Number: 2018953518

ISBN 978-1-4896-8028-0 (hardcover)

Printed in Brainerd, Minnesota,United States
1 2 3 4 5 6 7 8 9 0 22 21 20 19 18

082018
120917

Project Coordinators: John Willis
Designer: Mandy Christiansen

Weigl acknowledges Getty Images, Alamy, iStock, and Dreamstime as the primary image suppliers for this title.

EYEDISCOVER provides enriched content, optimized for tablet use, that supplements and complements this book. EYEDISCOVER books strive to create inspired learning and engage young minds in a total learning experience.

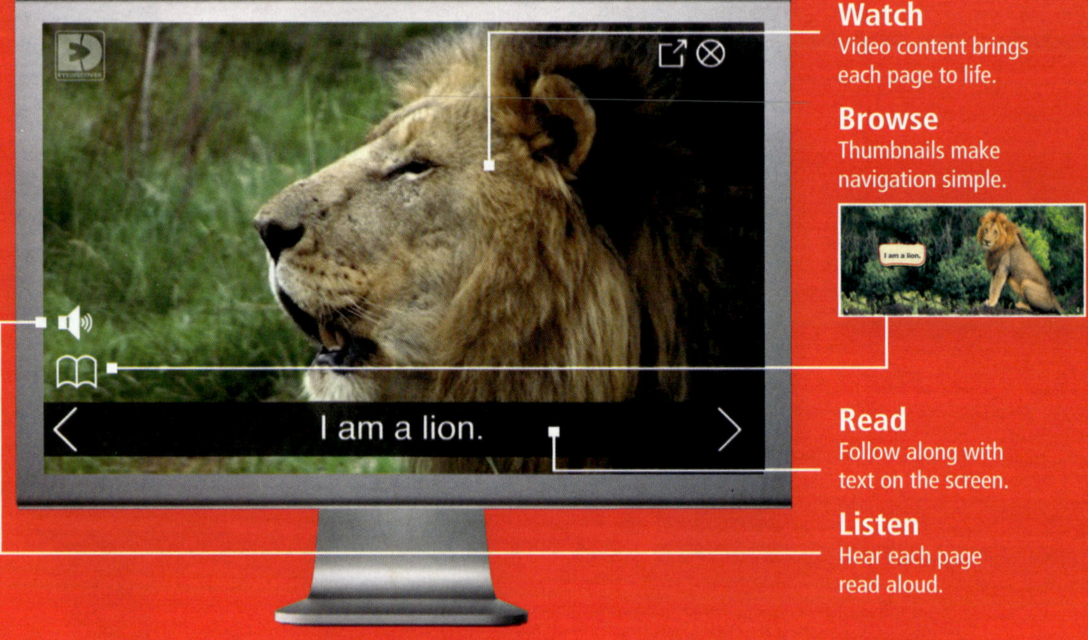

Watch
Video content brings each page to life.

Browse
Thumbnails make navigation simple.

Read
Follow along with text on the screen.

Listen
Hear each page read aloud.

Your EYEDISCOVER Optic Readalongs come alive with...

Audio
Listen to the entire book read aloud.

Video
High resolution videos turn each spread into an optic readalong.

OPTIMIZED FOR

- TABLETS
- WHITEBOARDS
- COMPUTERS
- AND MUCH MORE!

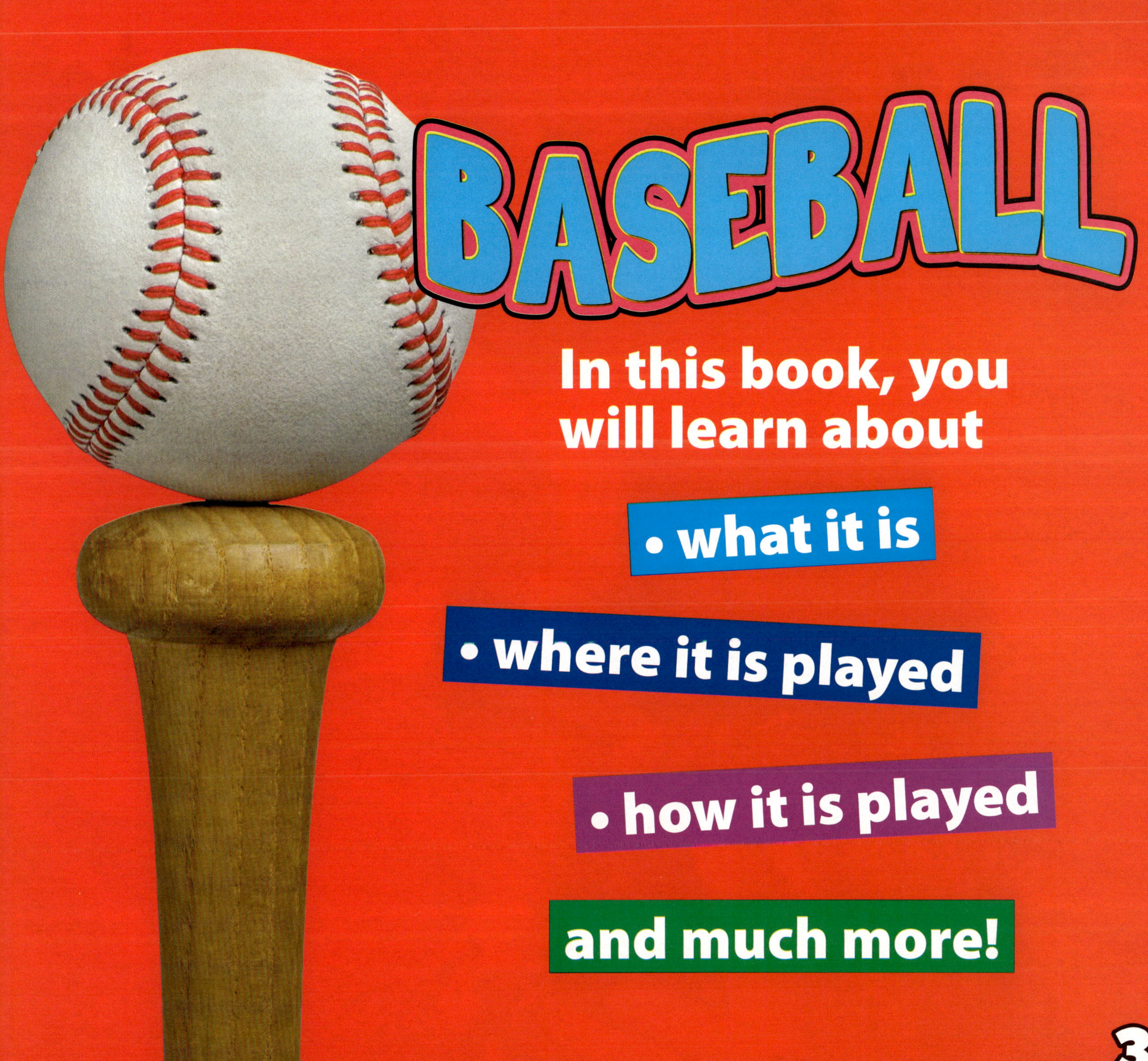

BASEBALL

In this book, you will learn about

- what it is
- where it is played
- how it is played

and much more!

4

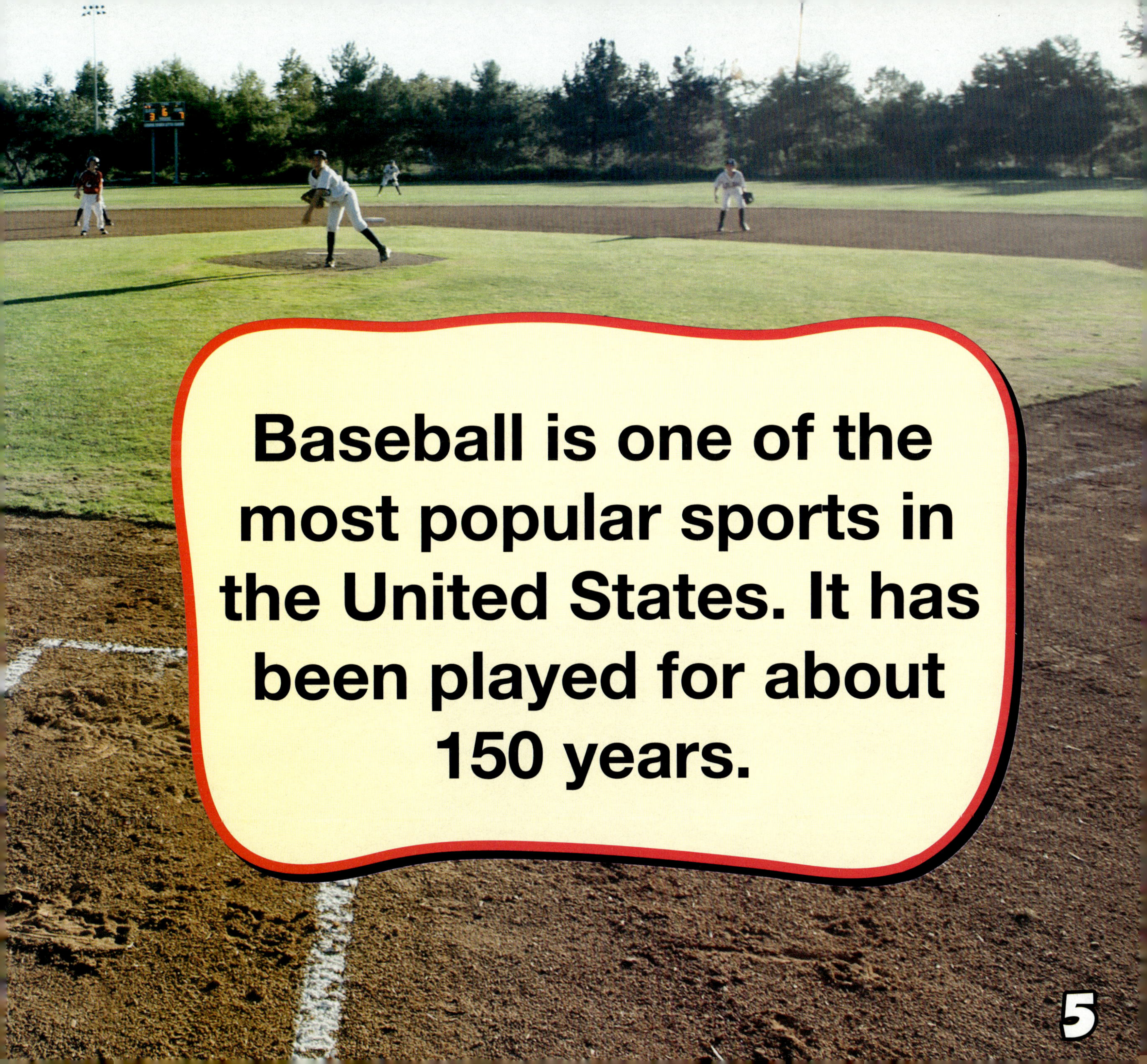

Baseball is one of the most popular sports in the United States. It has been played for about 150 years.

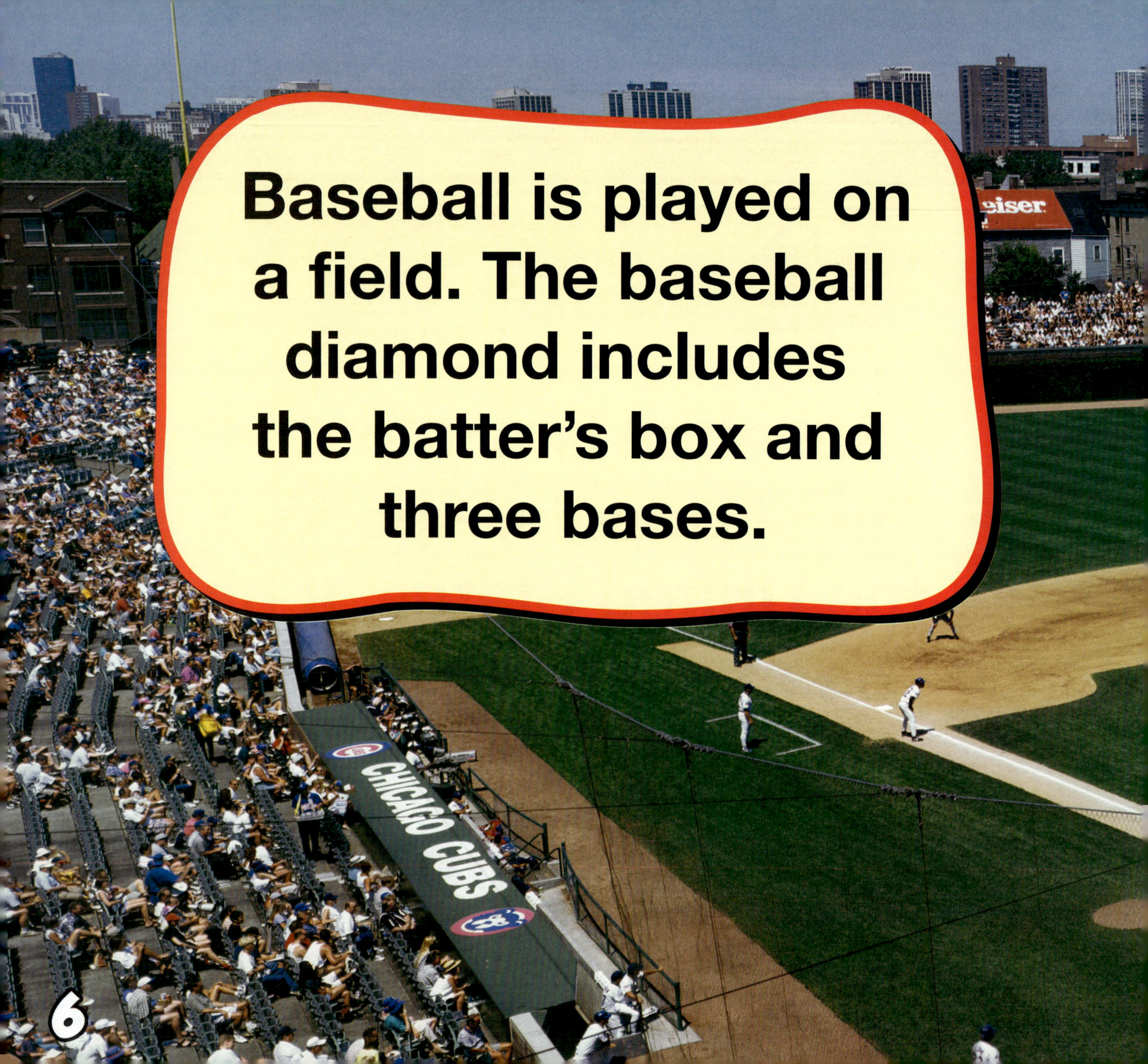

Baseball is played on a field. The baseball diamond includes the batter's box and three bases.

UMPIRES
AMERICAN
BATTER
SAMMY SOSA

The teams take turns at bat. Batters score a point by touching each base and making it back to home plate.

CARE FOR WHAT MATTERS
CARE FOR WHAT MATTERS

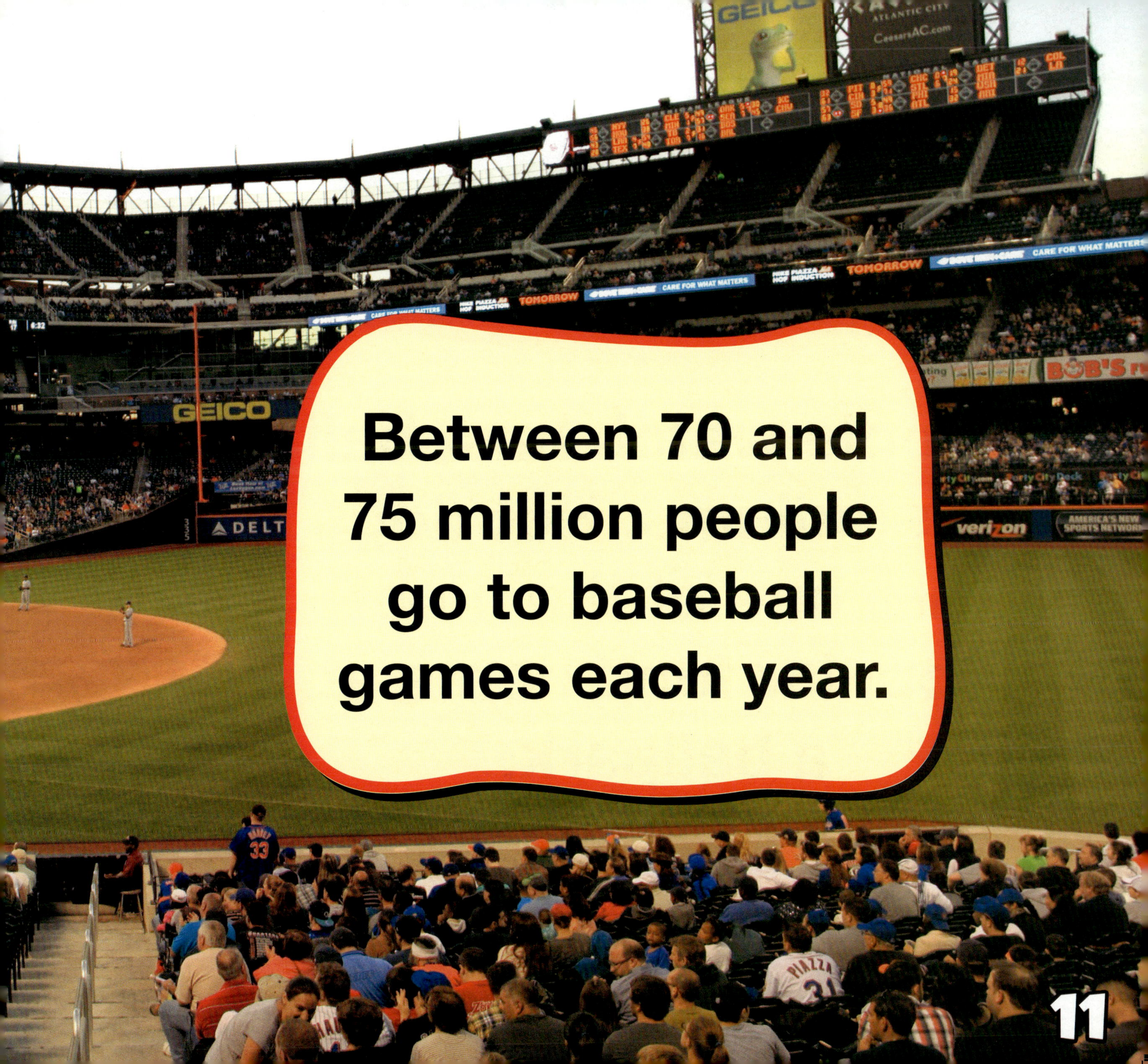

Between 70 and 75 million people go to baseball games each year.

People watch baseball in stadiums. Hot dogs are one of the most popular food items at a ballpark.

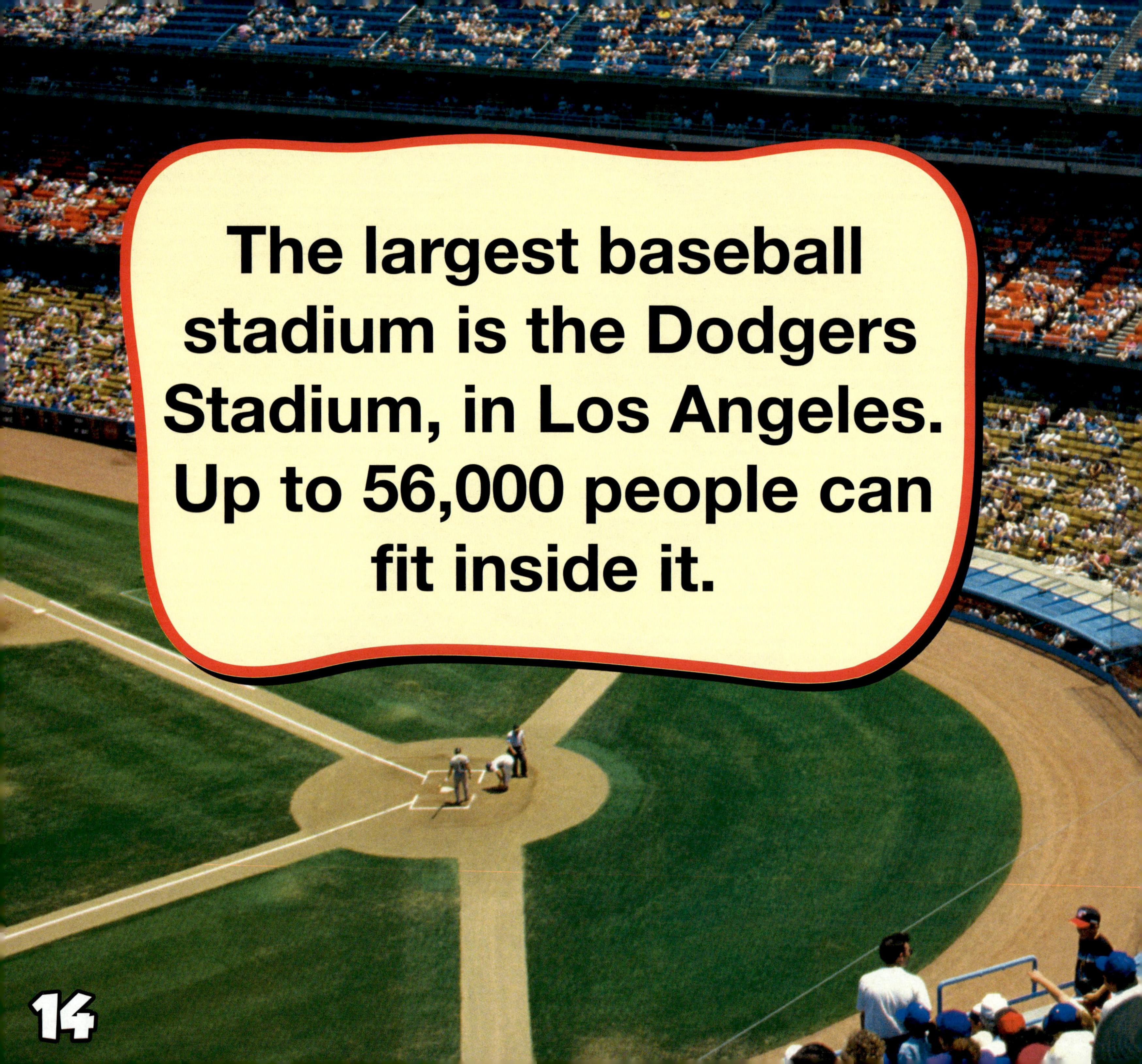

The largest baseball stadium is the Dodgers Stadium, in Los Angeles. Up to 56,000 people can fit inside it.

The best baseball players play in Major League Baseball. There are 30 MLB teams.

BH
BH

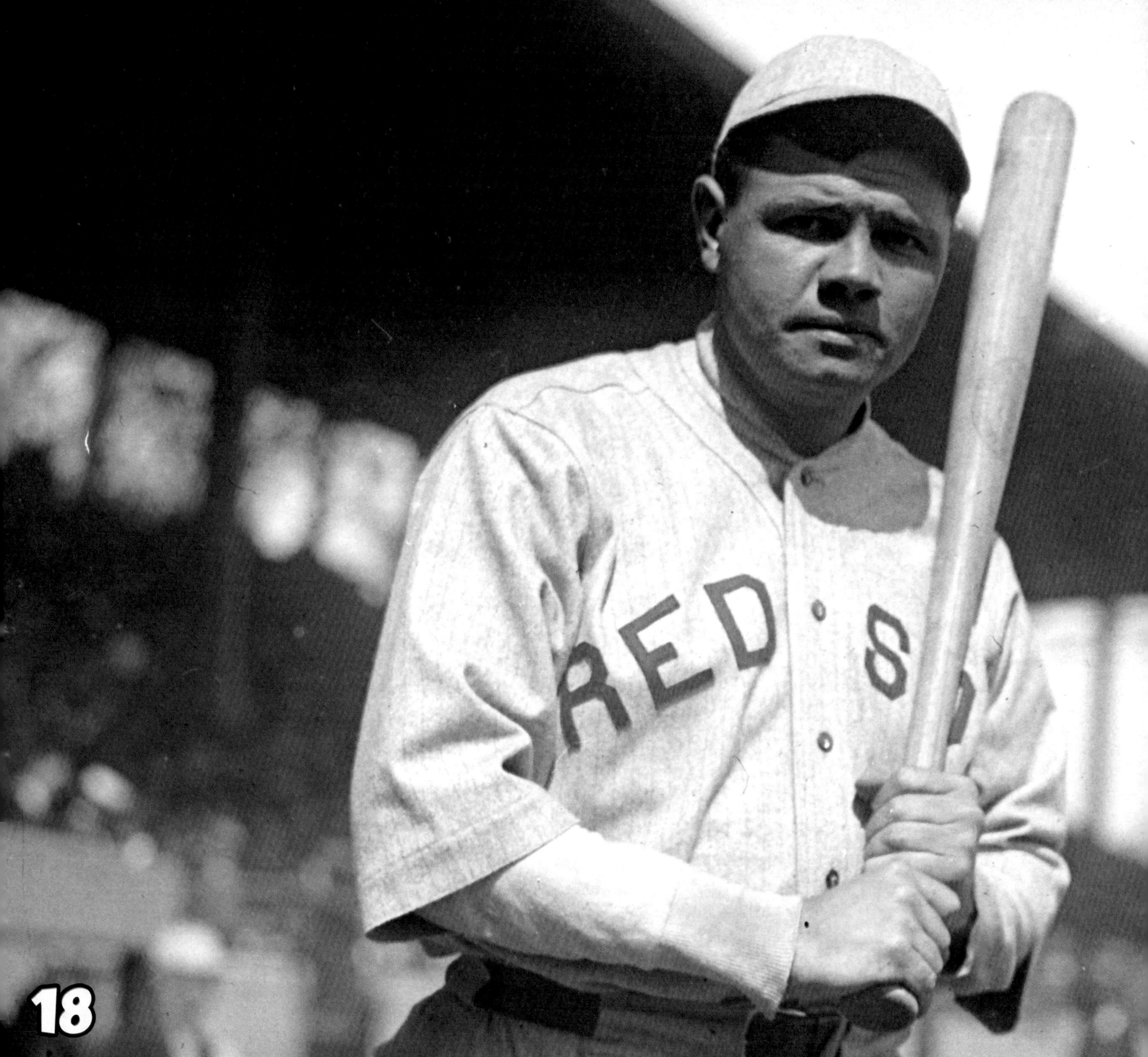
RED S

One of the best baseball players in history was named Babe Ruth. He was known for hitting home runs.

Baseball is a fun sport to both watch and play.

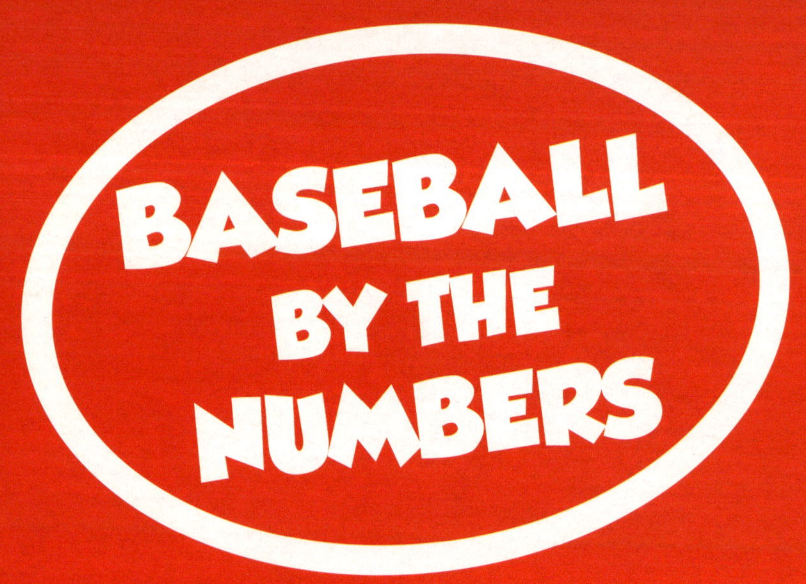

More than **19 million** hot **dogs** are sold to baseball fans each year.

In professional games, the baseball is replaced with a **new ball** every 5 to 7 pitches.

Today, more than **100 countries** have **professional** baseball teams.

The New York Yankees have won MLB's World Series 27 times.

The New York Yankees were the first MLB team to wear numbers on the backs of their jerseys.

Fenway Park, in Boston, Massachusetts, is the oldest MLB park still in use. It opened in 1912.

KEY WORDS

Research has shown that as much as 65 percent of all written material published in English is made up of 300 words. These 300 words cannot be taught using pictures or learned by sounding them out. They must be recognized by sight. This book contains 37 common sight words to help young readers improve their reading fluency and comprehension. This book also teaches young readers several important content words, such as proper nouns. These words are paired with pictures to aid in learning and improve understanding.

Page	Sight Words First Appearance
5	about, been, for, has, in, is, it, most, of, one, the, years
6	a, and, on, three
9	at, back, by, each, home, point, take, to
11	between, go, people
12	are, food, watch
14	can, up
16	play, there
19	he, was
20	both

Page	Content Words First Appearance
5	baseball, sports, United States
6	bases, batter's box, diamond, field
9	bat, home plate, teams
11	games
12	ballpark, hot dogs, stadiums
16	Major League Baseball
19	Babe Ruth, history

Watch
Video content brings each page to life.

Browse
Thumbnails make navigation simple.

Read
Follow along with text on the screen.

Listen
Hear each page read aloud.

Go to www.eyediscover.com and enter this book's unique code.

BOOK CODE

AVQ56868